Travelling Fair

Malcolm Slater

Japonica Press

First Published 2002

Copyright © Malcolm Slater 2002
The moral rights of the author have been asserted

All rights reserved. No parts of this publication may be reproduced, stored in a retrieval system, or transmitted, in any form or by any means, electronic, mechanical, photocopying, recording or otherwise, without prior permission of Japonica Press.

ISBN 0-9540222-2-X
UPC 9372700005

A catalogue record for this book is available from the British Library

Published by
Japonica Press
Low Green Farm, Hutton, Driffield,
East Yorkshire, YO25 9PX
United Kingdom

Cover design and book layout by Banks Design

Printed in Spain

Introduction

The subject of fairground transport is very interesting and diverse. 1969 was the year that I took up my camera and set out to record the fairground scene, with the emphasis on transport; I was soon hooked! In the late 1960s and 1970s transport consisted mainly of drawbar tractors and the eight wheeler rigid, particularly if the vehicle had a trusty Gardner engine under the bonnet. The thrill rides of the day were Dive Bombers and Twists. The Speedway, Dodgem and Waltzer were the backbone of any fair. All this was to rapidly change! The 1980s saw a move to one load operation.

Aluminium was to replace the traditional use of wood on many rides making them lighter and more transportable. Although the use of articulated fifth wheel units was not new, several showmen had been using them for many years, but it was in the late 1970s and early 1980s that the showmen turned to the fifth wheel in a big way. Construction and Use regulations introduced by governments made the move over to modern, faster vehicles even more of a necessity. Looking back, British made lorries ruled, and enthusiasts had to travel many miles to find a vehicle of foreign manufacture. I well remember seeing my first Scania 111 in fairground service with Yorkshire showman James Southward. This artic unit was somehow not quite the same as the Scammell Handyman unit it had replaced. There was nothing like a Scammell or Foden vehicle to point the camera at. The result was that I only ever took a few pictures of the Scania, which with the benefit of hindsight, was a bad mistake because today even that Scania model is history. The 80s and 90s saw the biggest changes in showman's transport. The 1980s saw a big decline in the British truck building market, with many firms facing closure being purchased by foreign competitors, and others being closed down altogether. Today foreign built vehicles are widely used by showmen.

The teenagers and public who visit our fairs no longer want to be frightened. Scaring them out of their skins is the order of the day and the showman has been quick to see this, investing huge sums of money in new fast thrill rides many of which are built overseas. It is not unusual to see a Roller Coaster at our larger fairs. These rides were confined to theme parks in the past because of the number of vehicles, trailers and even mobile cranes required to move them. British showmen now often operate their rides overseas. Dubai, Cyprus and Holland are just some of the countries showmen have opened in, and likewise foreign showmen have visited Britain often with rides new to our eyes.

Towards the end of the book I have included a short section on the showman's home. By the very nature of his business the fairground operator is always on the move and so his home has to be mobile. Living wagons are more than just caravans, and many can cost as much as a traditional house. Just as transport has changed, so has the living wagon. This book was never intended to be a detailed account of every make or model of vehicle that has done fairground service in Britain. It is more a personal look back at over 30 years of fair going and many of the vehicles I have encountered on the way.

Details are given in good faith and on the information given to me at the time by showmen and others. I am well aware that the showmen are very good at adapting vehicles to suit their needs and often vehicles are not what they appear at first sight; conversions are a common sight. Therefore some of the vehicles contained within these pages may have been wrongly credited, if this is so I apologise. I sincerely hope that you approve of my choice of photographs, which are only a small selection from a vast archive of material.

If you are new to the fairground scene you may like to know that there are two thriving societies dedicated to fairgrounds which you can join, or better still visit your local fair!

Malcolm Slater
July 1999.

AEC

RIGHT: AEC built more Matadors than any other model in their range. Raymond Armstrong's Matador lasted longer than most on the Notts & Derby fairground scene. It received modification to the front end whilst during service with Armstrongs, with the addition of a small bonnet to accommodate a larger engine and a one piece full width screen. The tractor was in use until the early 1990s. *Photograph by Graham Upchurch.*

RIGHT: Wilson's Amusements, Redditch had Matador FWP899 for many years. Fitted unusually with a Luton box body the vehicle was used with the firm's Dodgem ride. *Photograph by Rod Spooner.*

ABOVE AND RIGHT: It is still possible to find several Matadors working on fairground duties. One of the largest fleets still operating is that of the Harris family of Ashington, West Sussex. Matador WPX925F has received a replacement AEC Cab, and to help with the build up of the rides carries a modern hydraulic crane fitted on the rear of the chassis. Matador JPX70 carries a generating set on the rear. Note the modern AEC badges fitted to the radiator.
Both photographs by Les Freathy.

RIGHT: Some Matadors were fitted with rear twin wheels. Searles Amusements of Harlington used DGT8H, a twin wheeler, well into the 1980s with their Dodgem ride. Seen here at Wormwood Scrubs pull on.
Photograph by Malcolm Slater.

LEFT: Often referred to as six wheel Matadors, in fact AEC's model 0854 was a combination of a Marshall rear bogie and Matador front end. Built mainly as aircraft refuellers in World War 2 it was the only vehicle in AEC's stable not to receive a name. Thompson's 0854 is very lightly loaded carrying only one lighting set, and is seen here alongside the firm's four wheel Matador at Nottingham Goose Fair in 1971.
Photograph by Graham Upchurch.

RIGHT: AEC were from the start builders of buses. Showmen were quick to see the possibilities for adapting buses for their own use. Lowering the roof on a double decker or removing the upper floor, resulted in a vehicle capable of carrying large pieces of equipment. This early Regent model has seen better days, but even with damaged headlights the bus was still doing a useful job. *Photograph by late R. F. Mack.*

RIGHT: George Rowland's Mercury was fitted with the later Tillotson cab. The lorry was new to Cadbury's Chocolate, Bournville. Pictured here at the Brixham Regatta Fair pull on in 1984. *Photograph by Malcolm Slater.*

LEFT: Another Regent bus on fairground duties. Accommodation for staff has been built into the front lower deck. We are not quite sure what the AA would think if they were ever to be called out if the bus was to break down. The radiator carries an "AA" badge but it is doubtful if the vehicle ever received their assistance.

Photograph by late R. F. Mack.

BELOW: The AEC new medium weight truck introduced in the early 1950s was called the Mercury. It was designed for 12 tons gross weight and many found their way into fairground service. This one survived well into the 1970s and is seen here leaving Hull Fair. A few vehicles were still working into the 1990s.

Photograph by Malcolm Slater.

BELOW: Seen at Bath in 1987, Rodgers' Amusements' Mammoth Major V was used to carry part of the dodgem track with the cars on the lower deck and the nets from the ceiling on the upper. The lorry's Park Royal cab looks in very good condition for the vehicle's age.

Photograph by Malcolm Slater.

AEC

BELOW: A variant on the Mercury cab. NTM744 was operated by showman H. Rodgers. A side opening door aids loading and unloading, and the grill at the front of the body helps air circulation to the small generator. The large round disc propped up near the rear is the Swanne tank used on the Hook a Duck game. *Photograph by Malcolm Slater.*

ABOVE: AEC's 8 wheeler was known as the Mammoth Major. Tom Smith's Octopus ride was transported on this 1960 well lettered lorry. The second axle has been removed making the lorry look a little ungainly. The Octopus ride, along with the lorry, was sold to Gerry Cottle of circus fame whose name appears on the door and who used it for a short period on his Carnival Extravaganza Fun Fair and Circus. The ride was sold on once again, this time to John Carter's Fun Fair where it still operates together with the faithful AEC.
Photograph by Richard Laughton.

RIGHT: Northern Section showman Luke Jobson operated this Mammoth Major V with his Dodgem ride, attending many fairs on Teesside. The lorry was little changed from its haulage days.
Photograph by Paul Evans.

Travelling Fair

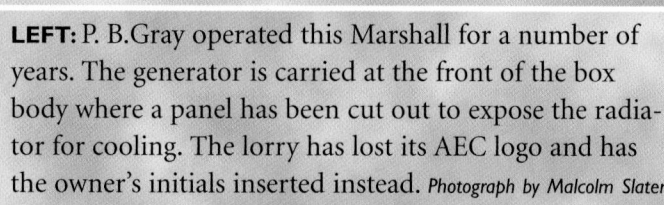

LEFT: P. B. Gray operated this Marshall for a number of years. The generator is carried at the front of the box body where a panel has been cut out to expose the radiator for cooling. The lorry has lost its AEC logo and has the owner's initials inserted instead. *Photograph by Malcolm Slater.*

RIGHT: L. Holden used this Mercury with the Ergo cab giving a clue to AEC's new owners Leyland, who took the company over in 1964. The lorry has been kitted out for its life on the fairground, with the addition of belly boxes and a stowage rack for the diesel drums. The Swanne tank from the Hook a Duck is carried between the cab and body. *Photograph by Malcolm Slater.*

LEFT: Arthur Owen Amusements were travelling a Flying Coaster ride during the 1980s. The ride was carried on this AEC Marshall which would seem to have been fitted with a later style Ergo cab from a Mercury model whose badge is still carried on the near side. The Flying Coaster itself was carried on the frame body and the two long girders protruding out from the rear were used to lift the machine centre on and off the rear end with the help of chain blocks. The girders could be stowed inside under the upper deck floor for transportation. The lorry was named Mathew after Arthur's son.

Photograph by Malcolm Slater.

LEFT: When Yorkshire showman Joseph Ling purchased a Waltzer he obtained this Marshal to carry the platforms. It is fitted with only the lightest of body work to help overcome weight problems when carrying the ride sections. A small centrally mounted crane helps with loading and unloading. *Photograph by Malcolm Slater*

ABOVE: J. Rowland & Son used this Marshall as a generating tractor with their Atlanta Dodgems travelling widely around Devon and Cornwall.
Photograph by Richard Laughton.

RIGHT: Although a product of British Leyland the AEC Mammoth Major was still being produced in the 1960s. This MM8 carries an additional badge, probably put there by its showman owner, which a collector would die for. The lorry carried a Twist ride within its curtain side body. It was pictured at Hampton Court Easter Fair.
Photograph by Malcolm Slater.

LEFT: Harry Fleming's Arcade travelled widely around the Yorkshire fairs, hauled by this AEC Mandator tractor. The lighting set is perched somewhat precariously behind the cab. The unit was photographed here leaving Hull Fair in the early 1980s.
Photograph by Malcolm Slater.

Albion

RIGHT: Albion's eight wheeler was known as the Caledonian. Some were turned out with the very distinctive Alfred Mile's cab. All went into service with Shell Petroleum. Lancashire section showman J. Silcock used two such vehicles. XPY163 was put into service with the firm's Waltzer and finished in the more familiar maroon livery of Silcocks. The other Caledonian XPY152 carried the Twist ride. The cab retained its yellow & white livery of Shell Mex/BP Ltd.
Photograph by Graham Upchurch.

BELOW: Ernest Ashcroft used this Albion Chieftain Super Six to transport his side stalls etc. The lorry and living wagon were photographed arriving at Owlerton Fair, Sheffield.
Photograph by Malcolm Slater.

RIGHT: Vintage Albion in the shape of A. C. Culine's box lorry at Harrogate Stray Fair in 1973. The lorry was first registered in Sunderland. Harrogate was the southern limit of Culine's travels. Standing next to the Albion is the Dennis Hefty of Bill Leach, this northern vehicle, having started its life with the Newcastle Co-Op. *Photograph by Malcolm Slater.*

ABOVE: Another Alfred Miles style Caledonian was operated again in Lancashire by J. Shaw and carried his Dodgem track. The lorry carried the floor of the ride and was retired in the mid 1970s after being replaced by another ex Shell tanker, this time a Scammell Routeman.
Photograph by Malcolm Slater.

LEFT: Another Albion Chieftain Super Six, this time photographed at Carlisle. The box body has been fabricated from a larger body with a side access door fitted.
Photograph by Malcolm Slater.

BELOW: Boyd's Skid ride was transported on this Albion Super Reiver 20. The cab of the lorry is showing signs of having had a hard fairground life, with various bumps and dents very much in evidence. The picture was taken at Hampstead Heath Easter Fair. *Photograph by Malcolm Slater*

ABOVE: Albion's Ergo cabbed Super Reiver. This Leeds registered lorry fitted with a Luton body, is a product of Leyland trucks who purchased Albion trucks in 1951. Note the hinged panel on the body over the cab, which opened up to allow the cab to be tilted for access to the engine. *Photograph by Malcolm Slater.*

Atkinson

LEFT: An Atkinson from the White's fleet. No 23 is a six wheeler first registered in Sunderland. Carrying the name The Saint the radiator seems to have acquired some extra Silver Knight Heads in the course of its travels around Scotland. *Photograph by Pete Tei.*

RIGHT: J. White's Amusements are well known north of the border. One of the first fairs of the season for White's is the famous Kirkcaldy Links Mart held in April. White's vehicles have always been lettered and finished to the highest standard, as this view of the firms Atkinson L15 model will testify. The lorry was used with White's Waltzer ride. *Photograph by Pete Tei.*

LEFT: New to Newcastle Breweries this Atkinson survived into the 1970s. Operated by showman Bernard Jeffreys it is seen here at the Northallerton May Fair in 1974. It was to be scrapped the following year. *Photograph by Malcolm Slater*

Travelling Fair

RIGHT: Another Atkinson survivor was that of Yorkshire section showman Jackie Bassett, in service into the 1970s. The cab style was introduced by Atkinsons in the 1930s and was common to all models well into the 1950s.
Photograph by Malcolm Slater.

RIGHT: Northern Section showman Billy Smith travels a darts stall. Billy's Atkinson Black Knight model was new to John Smith's Brewery, Tadcaster. The radiator carries a smaller Atkinson Badge so that it can also accomodate the magnet logo of John Smiths Magnet Ales.
Photograph by Malcolm Slater

ABOVE: Cumberland registered Black Knight received a very stylish body for its spell of fairground service. John Walker travelled the lorry around the Yorkshire fairs. Note the addition of the AA badge and lucky horse shoe to the radiator. *Photograph by Malcolm Slater.*

BELOW: Atkinson Silver Knight DVN999C started its life with Sunter Bros Heavy Haulage of Northallerton. It was sold by Sunters to showman Albert Evans who used it as a generating tractor fitted with showman's sides and a lighting set on the back. The tractor was to stay like this accompanying Albert's Jets ride for several years before being transferred to hauling the Waltzer ride. When one of the new generation of fold up Twist rides was purchased, the Atkinson was put back to its original fifth wheel guise to haul the ride, which is seen here at Bridlington on the Yorkshire coast.
Photograph by Malcolm Slater.

RIGHT: David Manning's Atkinson LRA 604D was used with his Hurricane Jets ride. The strengthening cross members above the body give added height, something to watch when moving near trees or low bridges. Full use has been made of the Atkis front panel to advertise its owners other ventures. *Photograph by Richard Laughton.*

LEFT: Harry Parrish travelled a Skid ride during the 1980s, attending many Yorkshire fairs including the big Hull fair in October. The ride was transported on a pair of Atkinson eight wheelers. EPD839B, first registered in Surrey, was named Moving On. The lorry was fitted with a crane on the front end, which was to assist with lifting the Skid cars on and off the track. "Moving On" is seen here at Woodhouse Moor Fair in Leeds. *Photograph by Malcolm Slater.*

RIGHT: John Scarrott travels widely around Northamptonshire. The fleet of vehicles used to transport his rides are split between Atkinson and ERF. All are finished to a very high standard and always immaculately turned out. CMG236A poses with the Dodgem load before setting off for the next fair. *Photograph by Richard Laughton.*

Atkinson

LEFT: In 1963 Atkinson built lorries specially designed for gritting and salting Britain's growing network of motorways. After retirement many of these 6x6 units found further service with fairground and circuses. One of these ex-motorway Atkinsons is used with showman John Carter with his Kings of Rock & Roll Dodgem track. Carrying lighting sets the tractor is named The Wanderer. *Photograph by Richard Laughton.*

RIGHT: One ex-motorway Atkinson used as a generator tractor, lost one of its rear axles for its life on the tober. This tractor was photographed at Hampton Court Easter Fair and travels widely around London with Rose Bros. Amusements. *Photograph by Malcolm Slater.*

BELOW: Another ex-motorway Atkinson has found a second life with John Coneley's Amusements. Lettered and lined the tractor hauls two trailers and makes an impressive sight on the move. *Photograph by Malcolm Slater.*

Travelling Fair

BELOW: Atkinson's version of the Scammell Highwayman. Only a handful of these bonneted tractors were built, all going to Pickford's Heavy Haulage. James Crow operated this unit well into the 1980s. It was No. M3444 in Pickford's fleet. The tractor is now in preservation. *Photograph by Malcolm Slater.*

LEFT: In 1966 Atkinson introduced the Viewline cab, a title that suited the vehicle well with its large screen. It seemed like a good idea, but not very driver friendly. Notice the high position of the door handle on this Viewline operated for many years by showman Stanley Thurston. Most of the Viewline models were sold to Pickford's Heavy Haulage when new. Several found their way onto the fairground circuit. *Photograph by Richard Laughton.*

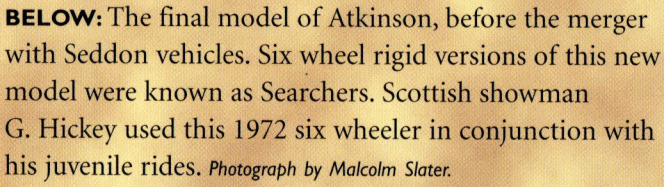

BELOW: Around 1963 the front styling of the cab was reused, but it never caught on, as operators favoured the traditional type of exposed radiator. White's Amusements operated two eight wheelers with the new styling in the 1980s. One was photographed here at the Kirkcaldy Links Mart Fair. *Photograph by Malcolm Slater.*

BELOW: The final model of Atkinson, before the merger with Seddon vehicles. Six wheel rigid versions of this new model were known as Searchers. Scottish showman G. Hickey used this 1972 six wheeler in conjunction with his juvenile rides. *Photograph by Malcolm Slater.*

LEFT: 27 years old and still going strong is Henry Hill's, eight wheel Defender. The lorry is a regular at many Lancashire fairs. As well as carrying the lighting set as can be seen, the lorry also carries a complete Twist ride. Henry is seen about to leave the 1998 Knutsford May Fair. *Photograph by Malcolm Slater.*

RIGHT: Robert Dailey's artic Twist load at Malton, North Yorkshire. Transport buffs will recognise the tractor unit's previous owners by the distinctive bull bar used on the front of all Ernest Thorpe, Sheffield transport. The Borderer tractive unit also carried the lighting set. The Twist ride was sold on in the early 1990s to a Scottish showman. *Photograph by Malcolm Slater*

LEFT: The following two pictures are of one of David Houghton's Waltzer load, part of which is carried on an Atkinson Defender. The ride and its attendant transport were previously with Alf Guess & Sons whose name it still carries in the light box. Unusually, the ride centre, normally carried on its own truck, is carried on the rest of the lorry. As one might expect with such a heavy weight UPJ had a tendency to try and dig itself down to Australia on soft and wet ground. *Photograph by Malcolm Slater*

Austin

RIGHT: The Austin 3 ton parcel van was introduced in 1958. Many hundreds were sold to BRS who had a part in the vehicle's design. Second hand vehicles were snapped up by many showmen, and you were almost certain to find one on any fairground. The vehicle pictured here was photographed at Hampstead Heath Easter Fair. *Photograph by Malcolm Slater.*

LEFT: The 3 ton Austins were known as Noddy Vans. The floor was a mere 3ft 3in. high and the body had a capacity of 600cu ft. This "Noddy Van" was photographed at Abingdon. *Photograph by Malcolm Slater.*

RIGHT: The Austin/BMC FF series was introduced towards the end of the 1960s. Several versions were available with either petrol or diesel engines. The 5 tonner was a popular model with the showmen. Caleb Johnson was using this Bradford registered box van in the 1970s. *Photograph by Malcolm Slater.*

ABOVE: V. Briggs was using this FF series in the late 1970s. This model featured a coach-built cab, presumably from its early days as a removal van. Holme upon Spalding Moor in East Yorkshire was one of a number of smaller villages which the family attended with juveniles as well as a Speedway ride. *Photograph by Malcolm Slater.*

BELOW: Lancashire showman Billy Bedford's FF series lasted well into the 1980s. The lorry was first registered in Oldham, Lancs and sports a Leyland badge added by its owner. *Photograph by Malcolm Slater.*

Bedford

RIGHT: Bedford's first forward control vehicle was the QL Military 3 tonner. Over 50,000 were built from 1941. It was inevitable that several would find their way onto the fairground when they became surplus to military requirements. The only "QL" operating with a British travelling fair during the 1990s was JAD902 owned by West Sussex showman Doug Harris. The original petrol engine has long since given way to a more economical diesel. Note the spade carried on the body, to help dig the lorry out of sticky situations, something the original would have carried way back in the 1940s.
Photograph by Les Freathy.

LEFT: Scott Pullen's Super Trooper was an upright Paratrooper ride, which was an articulated unit. A DAF tractor was used to move the ride from fair to fair. This Bedford TK model was used to carry the generators for the ride. The Bedford was painted in overall black livery with styled lettering to suit. The Bedford was later retired when the ride was fitted with a front dolly, enabling the lighting set to be carried on the DAF which was now used as a drawbar tractor. *Photograph by Malcolm Slater.*

RIGHT: Bedford introduced the OB coach in 1939. The coach seen in this picture JAE449 is a model OWB first introduced in 1942. R. Saunders has been a long-time user of coach and bus chassis for his fairground Fish & Chip bars. Several of the ex Saunder's vehicles have now been preserved.
Photograph from the Glen McBirnie collection.

LEFT: Bedford supplied chassis to specialist body builders. First registered in the 1970s, this radiography unit was used in the Hull area. On retirement it was acquired by a showman and converted into a mobile home. Photographed at Newcastle Town Moor. *Photograph by Malcolm Slater.*

ABOVE: The Bedford TK range was available in many variations, most of which found favour with showmen. Coupland's operated one of the largest catering units and travelled widely across the country in the 1980s. This small tractor unit was in charge of the catering unit for a long time and is seen here at the famous Town Moor Hoppings, Newcastle. *Photograph by Malcolm Slater.*

LEFT: The KM series covered a higher weight range and this KM carries the Fun House, popular with children as well as adults. *Photograph by Malcolm Slater.*

ABOVE: The TL range has a distinct look of the earlier TK's and features a tilt cab. Stevens's chip bar is seen here at Battersea in London. The lorry is towing another catering trailer.
Photograph by Malcolm Slater.

BELOW: Launched in 1974 the TM was available in two cab styles. Artic tractor units are hard to find operating with showmen. One showman J. Danter had this F cab TM hauling his Turbo Twist ride for a period in the 1980s. *Photograph by Malcolm Slater.*

LEFT: BMC were formed in 1952 following the merger of Austin and Morris. The British Motor Corporation badged a few vehicles BMC before they were in turn purchased by Leyland.
The FG range of vans and light trucks was launched in 1959 by BMC. Many went into fairground service some continuing well into the 1990s. This BMC badged FG was spotted on Woodhouse Moor in Leeds early in 1983.
Photograph by Malcolm Slater.

LEFT: In 1968 the Laird was introduced onto the British truck market. It was available as a 9.6 to 12 ton vehicle. The cab was built in Bathgate and was known as the G cab. A former removals van based on a Laird chassis makes an ideal vehicle for moving small juvenile rides and stalls. The lorry has been named Louise presumably after a daughter of the owner.
Photograph by Malcolm Slater.

RIGHT: A BMC Laird arriving at Nottingham Goose Fair. As well as the BMC badge the cab also has a square Leyland badge giving away the vehicle's parentage. The lorry has a small generator in the front of the body and the exhaust carries the fumes from the working set high above the fairground when operating. *Photograph by Malcolm Slater.*

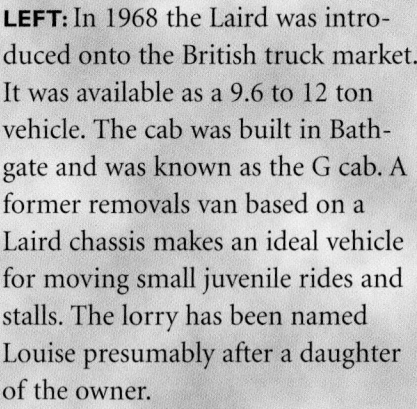

Bristol

LEFT: The Bristol Tramways & Carriage Company are well known for the buses that they produced, although they did manufacture some lorries mainly for BRS. Bus chassis were once very popular with showmen. This former bus has received a complete makeover for its life on the fairground, including a new full width cab and box body. It was once with United buses and was photographed at Woolwich Common Fair in 1959. *Photograph by Rod Mullard.*

ABOVE: This Bristol J retained its looks for its life with the fun fair. It started its life with United Automobile Services. *Photograph by late Robert Mack*

RIGHT: G. R. Tucker's yard in winter with snow on the ground. Tuckers had this 1937 Bristol J operating for many years after its first owners United Automobile Services had retired it. As can be seen from the photograph, apart from the addition of greedy boards on the roof, the basic outside appearance of the bus is little changed.

Photograph by late Robert Mack.

Bristol

BELOW: This single decker Bristol which only made a brief appearance with the travelling fai was owned by Gooch's. Part of the saloon has been removed to accomodate a beaver tail, thus enabling the family car to be carried. Photographed at Newcastle Town Moor in the 1980s.

Photograph by Malcolm Slater

ABOVE: Virtually extinct from the 1990's fairground is the converted bus used as a means of transporting equipment. However there are a few around still giving yeoman service. This 1938 Bristol, operated by John Carter's Fun Fair, Maidenhead, is almost definitely the oldest still in service with a fun fair. The bus has been converted to living accommodation and is in regular working service with Carter's.

Photograph by Malcolm Slater.

Travelling Fair

Commer

RIGHT: This Commer Maxiload, formerly a removals van in York, has had a Fun House fitted to the original body. Owned by Tommy Peel the "Ghost Manor" as the attraction was known, travelled the Yorkshire Fairs and was very popular with children.
Photograph by Malcolm Slater.

LEFT: Another Maxiload, this time operating in and around Lancashire with J. Thwaites of Salford. The large box body accommodates the side stalls.
Photograph by Malcolm Slater.

RIGHT: The Commer Maxiload was available in weight ranges from 8 to 16 tons with a variety of wheelbase lengths. There can be no mistake as to where this Maxiload travels, as the front panel proclaims "Frae the Borders." The Edinburgh registered van is with "Bingo Bob" Miller at Carlisle. The cab style is known as the CA. *Photograph by Malcolm Slater.*

ABOVE: The Commer Walk thru Van was available as either a 1.5 ton model or as a 2 ton version, which was fitted with twin rear wheels. This 2 ton version seen at Kirkcaldy Fair, north of the border had been fitted as a Fish and Chip bar. *Photograph by Malcolm Slater.*

BELOW: One of the most successful designs was the 100-series Commando. This model is actually a product of the Chrysler Corporation which took over the Rootes group makers of Commer vehicles in the 1960s. Early models were badged as Commer. HSW801P had been used for bakery deliveries before being acquired for further service on the fairground. *Photograph by Malcolm Slater.*

Crane's

BELOW: Not all showmen choose to travel, many have settled down at seaside sites and operate fairground equipment rides etc. on a permanent basis. R&S Amusements operate several rides on Blackpool's South Pier as well as running arcades in the town. One of the machines operated on the pier is a Miami ride. Built by ride manufacturers Notts UK Ltd., the services of a 200 ton crane were required to lift the machine onto the pier from the beach. The ride is seen during its lift in May 1999.
Photograph by Malcolm Slater.

ABOVE: When Matt Taylor purchased a Looping Star Roller Coaster it attended several of our larger fairs. The ride came along with this M.A.N. Tractor fitted with a hydraulic crane which was used to build up the ride. The M.A.N F range was available on the British truck market. *Photograph by Malcolm Slater.*

ABOVE: Dutch showmen have been regular attenders at the Belfast Christmas Fun Fairs. The rides they bring have been getting bigger and bigger as the years go by. A giant wheel is now a fairly common sight on our larger fairgrounds. Several British showmen have now purchased giant wheels and travel them quite successfully. The method of erecting these wheels can vary depending on the maker. Early models required the services of a large mobile crane, which often travelled with the wheel from fair to fair as can be seen with this Dutch showman arriving in Belfast. The crane is mounted on a DAF 2500 eight legger which pulls its owner's living wagon. *Photograph by Phillip Dunhill.*

BELOW: The name of William Bird & Sons is synonymous with travelling fairs in Ireland. Among the firm's large collection of rides is a Looping Roller Coaster, which travels with the fair. This is a type of ride that you would normally associate with permanent theme parks. To help with the build up of the coaster Birds use a Grove Coles AT5285 mobile crane and a Foden S106 fitted with a Palfinger hydraulic crane. The crane is moved from fair to fair on its own low loader trailer.

Both pictures were taken at the large Funderland Fair in Cork. The Coles is about to lift the Loop up into position on the coaster, whilst the Foden is about to fit the lift chain onto the coaster's first rise. *Photograph by Pod.*

DAF

RIGHT: A mid 1970s DAF FT 2200. This model featuring the F Series cab, which was to open up the British market for DAF built vehicles. This early tractor carries a generator for the single Dive Bomber load. The Dive Bomber ride was patented in 1938 in the United States. It consists of a vertical rotating arm with a rotating car on each end, giving a sensation of diving and looping. *Photograph by Malcolm Slater.*

LEFT: Based at Wigston near Carlisle, Slater's amusements travelled this left hand drive DAF 2000. The stylish pantechnicon still carry's its continental number plate and TIR identification. It was photographed at Wooler in Northumberland. *Photograph by Malcolm Slater.*

RIGHT: Arthur Holland travelled a Matterhorn ride during the early 1990s. The cab was restyled by DAF for the 2300 series. It was first registered in Shrewsbury in 1980 and is seen here arriving in Nottingham for the Goose Fair. *Photograph by Malcolm Slater.*

DAF

ABOVE: The 1990s saw the move to one load rides. Several machine manufacturers built one load Waltzers, whilst many showmen chose to convert their own machines to the one load configuration. This DAF 2800 tractive unit was developed from a Leyland design.
The 2800 was fitted with a 11.6 litre engine developing 276hp. The photograph was taken at the pull on for the Epsom Derby Fair. *Photograph by Malcolm Slater.*

ABOVE: Many showmen purchase second hand rides from overseas. Several rides which have entered this country have come complete with their attendant vehicles, resulting in vehicle models which would not normally be available here appearing on the British market. Some have only lasted a short time before being replaced by a more conventional vehicle.
Scottish showman Matt Taylor imported a Looping Roller Coaster ride and with it came this DAF 1900/2000 series dating from the 1960s. The lorry travelled for a couple of years, its latter duties being to move the Paratrooper ride.
Photograph by Malcolm Slater.

LEFT: In 1964 DAF launched the 2600 series cab. This new style cab is credited with setting standards of style and comfort which other manufacturers then followed. Early models were badged 304 denoting the engine horse power, however this badge was later removed after a complaint from Peugeot who said that it infringed their trade mark. The 2600 DAF cab was available on the British market and several found their way into fairground service.
Photograph by Richard Laughton.

RIGHT:
The British fairground scene has been opened up by showmen visiting from overseas, wanting to try their luck with rides new to Britain. This DAF 2300 series came over with a Dutch showman for the Kirkcaldy Links Fair. The small flat body is fitted with a hydraulic crane to help aid the build up. The body carried the machine paybox when on the road. The lorry was more for pulling than carrying. *Photograph by Malcolm Slater.*

Travelling Fair

RIGHT: Dennis are perhaps better known for their fire engines and municipal vehicles.
There cannot be many ex-county council refuse wagons that have found their way into fairground service, however, one was spotted at Wansted Flats Easter Fair in London. This Pax V model has retained its crew cab and received a curtain side body. *Photograph b Malcolm Slater.*

BELOW: Corrigan's Amusements travelled widely around North and East Yorkshire. For a period in the 1950s they operated a grass cutter Twist ride, part of which packed onto this London registered Dennis. Also in use at the time was a Foden FG model. Note the exhaust sack reaching high above the frame body work. *Photograph by Ernest Brown.*

RIGHT: J. Coupland operated this 1970s Pax V. Seen at the Townmoor Hoppings the towing tractor carried the lighting sets. The sign writer's art is shown to the full: the tractor was named Bandit after the film *"Smokey and the Bandit."*
Photograph by Malcolm Slater

BELOW: Dennis were builders of buses as well as lorries and the Lancet was perhaps the most famous model. This showmanised "Lancet" seems little changed from its passenger carrying days. No doubt all the seats will have been removed to make way for the fairground equipment and a roof top storage box completes the scene. Alongside stands a Maudslay Mogul box lorry.
Photograph by late Robert Mack..

Dodge

RIGHT: The proprietary Motor Panel's cab was fitted to Dodge trucks in the 1960s. John Newsome operated this vehicle around Teeside. However it was in Harrogate, North Yorkshire that this photograph was taken in the early 1970s. *Photograph by Malcolm Slater.*

LEFT: The Rootes group Hi Line cab was fitted to the Commer Commando. This Dodge badged Hi-Line Commando was operated in South Yorkshire by Pullin Bros. The brothers travelled two large rides namely a Big Wheel and later a Dodgem ride around Sheffield and the West Riding. *Photograph by Malcolm Slater.*

RIGHT: Changed little from its days with British Telecom this Dodge Commando carries its original Papworth bodywork. *Photograph by Malcolm Slater.*

LEFT: Not many showmen bother with their own publicity vehicle but rely on poster or press advertising instead. Rose Bros Fun Fairs have this Dodge Commando engaged in publicity work for the fair. No one can say that they have not seen its large hoarding proclaiming where the fun fair is that week. *Photograph by Malcolm Slater.*

RIGHT: A Dodge Commando fitted with the later wide grill and what looks like an ex-Telcom body. The water tank from the Hook a Duck game is tied somewhat precariously on top of the body.
Photograph by Malcolm Slater.

LEFT: The 300 series Dodge represented the largest truck in Dodge's stable. It was available both as a tractor unit with a weight range from 30 to 38 tons and as an eight wheeler tipper. Few were sold in the tractor form and as a result only a handful found their way into fairground service. One exception was this 1978 Essex registered 38 tonner, which for several years was a regular attender at the Wanstead Flats Easter Fair.
Photograph by Malcolm Slater.

LEFT: The Dodge 500 series truck was produced from 1965 to 1976 and was available with a 13 ton to 28 ton chassis. This 1972 model is fitted with a very long box body, ideal for packing away those stalls etc.
Photograph by Malcolm Slater.

Ebro

ABOVE: A rare vehicle on any fairground in Britain is Holland's Ebro L75 model. Ebro trucks were made in Spain by a Ford subsidiary. A serious effort was made in the 1980s to import Ebro vehicles. They were sold by the British Nissan Organisation. Some were sold to councils and were used as street cleaners etc. Sales were discontinued towards the end of the 1980s. The photograph was taken at the Knutsford (Cheshire) May Day Fair.
Photograph by Malcolm Slater.

LEFT: Michael Holland's B series 2TR tractor unit was used to haul his living wagon. Michael travelled a set of Dodgems in Yorkshire and around Lincolnshire. The tractor unit was once with Eling transport. The outfit was wending its way through Huddersfield when the photograph was taken. *Photograph by Malcolm Slater.*

BELOW: George T. Tuby is one showman who ceased travelling to concentrate on his amusement arcades on the Yorkshire coast and the Luna Park at the seaside resort of Scarborough. Many travelling rides are operated at the Luna Park and George has introduced several new rides, one of which was a Top Spin. Although the ride stayed on the park throughout the summer, it did however leave the park at the end of the holiday season to attend some of the local back end fairs. One of the first fairs that it attended was the large September Fair held on the coach park in its home town of Scarborough. This ERF was put into service to move the ride during its back end run. The ride was sold and replaced by a Miami which itself has travelled away from its home base in Scarborough. *Photograph by Malcolm Slater.*

BELOW: Irvins' Dodgem load waiting for the Thame pull on in Berkshire. The Dodgem is one of the new generation of fold up tracks which are becoming very popular with operators. All the track is contained on the one load and folds out for build up. Some of the floor panels can be seen on the bottom of the ride. The dodgem cars themselves have to be carried on a separate vehicle, in this case an eight wheel Foden.

Photograph by Malcolm Slater.

RIGHT: Notts & Derby showman Frank Hall's ERF C15 model was the oldest working fairground ERF in the 1980s. The Luton box body was later changed for a roller sided box body, giving the lorry a much more compact look. New to Colbourn's Transport in 1944, Frank retired the vehicle towards the end of the 1980s for bodywork repairs, with a view to returning it to service. So far, however, it has not reappeared.
Photograph by Malcolm Slater.

ABOVE: Scotland was thought to have the oldest working ERF in 1998. The lorry was new to Hugh Harper & Sons in 1950. It is fitted with a box body and normally can be seen hauling a juvenile ride.
Photograph by Malcolm Slater.

LEFT: George Breeze used this KV model well into the 1970s. Used to travel his Side and Round stalls around Yorkshire fairs, the lorry was new to Mackintosh's Toffees, Halifax.
Photograph by Malcolm Slater.

LEFT: A. Payne's KV was another long survivor lasting into the late 1970s. The lining applied to the green livery and the skirt gave the lorry an elegant look.
Photograph by Malcolm Slater.

LEFT: Looking smart as ever. J. White & Sons eight Legger which was used to carry the Cyclone Twist ride when photographed in 1970.
Photograph by Pete Tei.

RIGHT: David Lings ERF survived long enough to be preserved after its working fairground days. The lorry's fairground duties involved transporting part of the Thriller Speedway ride. The ride was sold on without the transport, the lorry staying with Lings out of use. New in 1961 to Ibbotsons the vehicle is now restored as a tanker and is regularly rallied. *Photograph by Malcolm Slater.*

RIGHT: Glen Miller's Snake Slide travelled on one load. The lorry travelled widely and is seen here on the promenade at Kirkcaldy. The ride was built by Chris Randall Designs of Driffield East Yorkshire. The firm was a prolific builder of this type of ride.

The ride and lorry were sold to Cubbin's Amusements in Lancashire. The lorry was finally taken out of service in the winter of 1998/99. The ride is now carried on a more modern ERF. *Photograph by Malcolm Slater.*

LEFT: Still going strong in 1999, Chas Wright's Jets ride is carried on this ERF, chassis No 22874. The lorry was formerly a tipper operating in and around South Yorkshire. The Jets ride itself is rare on today's fairground, people preferring the white knuckle type of ride. The ride requires the use of an air compressor in order to lift the individual cars. Photographed at Knutsford May Fair. *Photograph by Malcolm Slater.*

ABOVE: John Scarrott's ERF was new in 1963 to Valentine Ord & Nagle Ltd. Often referred to as an A series its true model no. is 6.8GX3. The lorry is very lightly loaded for a showman's vehicle, retaining its flat body. Since retirement from fairground duties the lorry has been acquired for preservation. *Photograph by Richard Laughton.*

BELOW: Tommy Green's Scrambler ride is carried on this B series ERF. Lighting set as well as the complete ride are carried on the lorry which started life as a block carrier with Best Blocks in 1977. The outfit is seen here arriving at Knutsford towing one of Tommy's juvenile rides. *Photograph by Malcolm Slater.*

LEFT: J. W. Jameson's Foden DG. The lorry is ex-Ministry of Supply. The Foden 10 ton truck was built by Foden's for the war effort. John Jameson and family were still travelling in the 1990s with a Dodgem track, Fun House etc. Foden vehicles still feature strongly in the current fleet. *Photograph by Malcolm Slater.*

BELOW: William Coates DG model. Travelling north of the border, the lorry carried Round Stalls etc. Finished unusually for a showman in two tone blue, the lorry survived long enough to be preserved. *Photograph by Pete Tei.*

ABOVE: J. Whites Foden DG finished in maroon and lettered to the highest standard. The lorry worked with the Dodgem track. Glasgow registered, the vehicle was nearly 20 years old when this picture was taken in 1970. Note the headlamps mounted on the front cross member. *Photograph by Pete Tei.*

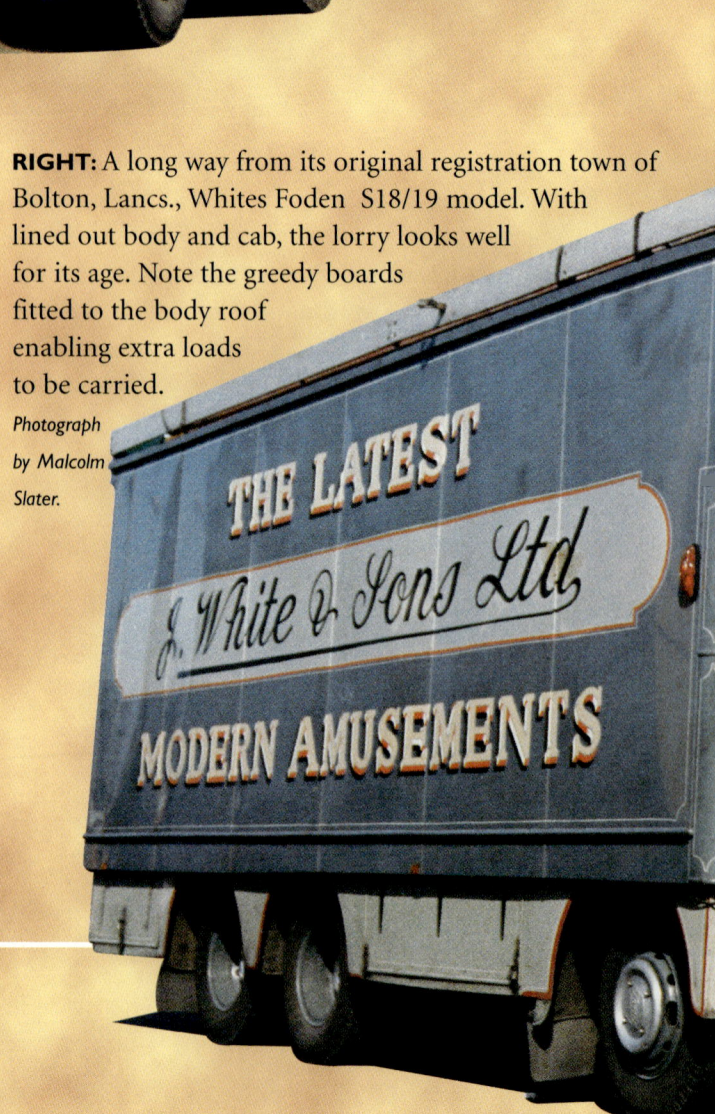

RIGHT: Foden FG No 9 in John Codona's fleet. As can be seen the lorry is used to transport the Super Waltzer ride. Lettered in finest showman tradition, the lorry was first registered in Manchester.
Photograph by Pete Tei

BELOW: Yorkshire showman Ernest Atha favoured Foden vehicles to transport both his large rides. This Foden S20 model was used with the small speedway ride. PUJ Started its life with Bison Floors and lasted well into the 1980s, being fitted later in life with a full box body.
Photograph by Malcolm Slater.

RIGHT: A long way from its original registration town of Bolton, Lancs., Whites Foden S18/19 model. With lined out body and cab, the lorry looks well for its age. Note the greedy boards fitted to the body roof enabling extra loads to be carried.
Photograph by Malcolm Slater.

Foden

LEFT: Foden vehicles have always found favour with showmen, especially if fitted with the trusty Gardner engine. Several Foden S20s lasted well into the 1980s and 90s some 30 years after this model was withdrawn from production. This pair of eight leggers stood the test of time.
Photograph by Richard Laughton.

RIGHT: Foden also produced a few bus chassis although they were not however as popular as their lorries and production only lasted until 1956. One coach UMP291, a PVSC 6 model, found its way into fairground service and is seen here little changed from its coaching days with Len Bibby in London during the 1960s.
Photograph by Paul Redfern.

BELOW: Graham Camfield's Foden FG ran well into the 1970s before retirement, where it remained until scrapped. From the look of the bodywork above the rear wheel, changing wheels could present a problem as there seems to be no removable panel. *Photograph by Malcolm Slater*

Travelling Fair

RIGHT: Trent embankment Nottingham and J. White's Big Wheel ride. The ride was transported with this Foden S20 six wheeler, the six wheel chassis was widely used as the basis for truck mixers. The lorry was used as a towing tractor and carried the lighting sets. *Photograph by Graham Upchuch*

LEFT: This Foden S20 started life as a recovery vehicle for Kent County Council. The tractor stayed basically the same for its spell of fairground service; only the recovery crane was removed and the winch was retained. The tractor is seen arriving at the Mitcham Statis Fair in 1996. *Photograph by Malcolm Slater.*

RIGHT: Hebborn's Amusements based in Oxford, had this Foden S21 model tractor with their Dodgem track. The lorry had probably been a concrete mixer before being converted to the generating tractor. The Foden S21 introduced by Fodens in 1957 set new standards in cab design, and was the first fibre glass cab produced by the company. *Photograph by Malcolm Slater*

Foden

LEFT: Harry Marshall's Foden Mickey Mouse S21, arriving at Hull for the giant Hull Fair. The Maxwell built ride could open either as a Waltzer or a Speedway depending on the fair it was attending. The ride now resides in a South Wales amusement park. *Photograph by Malcolm Slater*

LEFT: Culine's Teesside Amusements had two Foden S21 models travelling with their Speedway and later on their Waltzer. The lorries had consecutive registration numbers. 883 HUP retained its original flat body for its fairground life.

Photograph by Paul Evens

RIGHT: Following on from the S34 came the S36. Basically the same, the small headlights were replaced by twin headlamps. The cab of the S36 did not tilt. This vehicle operating in Scotland was ex-Robson's Border Transport, Carlisle. Although carrying the name Border Romany, the actual name credited to the vehicle's registration number was Border Princess. Originally a four wheel artic it was converted to a long wheelbase lorry by its showman owner. *Photograph by Malcolm Slater.*

Travelling Fair

ABOVE: Bert Holland's Foden S34 model with the owner's Arcade. The S34 model was produced when British truck builders were leaders. It was Foden's first truck with a tilt cab, but the design did not find favour with operators due to the small square headlamps. Many showmen removed the original lights and fitted the more conventional round light for better visibility during night moves.
Photograph by Malcolm Slater.

ABOVE: Following on from the S36 came the S39. This model with its split windscreen suited tipper operators who feared breakages with the single screens of the previous models. The S39 stayed in production the longest. Seen here is an extra long vehicle operated by showman Les Robson, which carried all of his Speedway/Ark ride. The ride itself was the rare five hill machine.
Photograph by Malcolm Slater

BELOW: John Crick's Skid travelled widely, spending much of the time in Yorkshire. The Foden S39 generating tractor was fitted with a front mounted crane which was used to lift the heavy Skid cars on and off the track. The trailer being towed behind the living wagon carries the family car. The photograph was taken in Walton Street, Hull. The houses and the stone mason's yard have all now gone, their place taken by old people's bungalows.
Photograph By Malcolm Slater

Foden

RIGHT: Northern Showman John Murphy acquired this Foden for use with his Waltzer ride. The lorry is one of the specialist vehicles built by Foden's for the Military. With low profile cab and underslung headlights, the body was transferred from the previous vehicle onto the new chassis cab. It is thought that this vehicle was unique in fairground service in the 1990s. *Photograph by Malcolm Slater*

LEFT: The Foden S80 model featured very large headlights, unlike other models before it. The 1974 tractor unit had a nomadic fairground life, having been with several owners together with its Twist load. It was photographed here at Hamilton in Scotland.
Photograph by Malcolm Slater

LEFT: One S40 that received a complete make over was TPT377K. This heavy haulage tractor saw service with Robert Oliver Heavy Haulage of Bishop Auckland. It was obtained by showman John Crow of Seaburn to accompany his Galloper ride. The tractor only ran for a short while, before it received a rebuild; a more modern Fleetmaster cab replaced the original, and the lighting sets were enclosed by a box body. The tractor was still running in 1999.
Photograph by Richard Laughton.

RIGHT: The Foden S40 saw a return to a steel cab for Fodens. Built by Motor Panels not many entered fairground service. This one was with Rose Bros Fun Fairs for several years, pulling one of the living vans.
Photograph by Malcolm Slater

Travelling Fair

RIGHT: Another of Foden's specialist vehicles was the 6x6 chassis for snow clearing on Britain's motorways. It carried a gritter spreader body and snow plough and a few eventually found their way onto the fairground. This one was with Steven's Amusements.
Photograph by Richard Laughton

LEFT: An elderly Foden S95 Fleetmaster tractor arrives at Cleethorpes with a trailer mounted Snake Slide. The S95 tractor was a high specification vehicle. The cab, built by Motor Panels, has wide doors and was made of steel.
Photograph by Malcolm Slater

RIGHT: After the Foden S80/83 models Foden went back to the S10 cab. J.W. Hatwell's roller powered tractor pulled the Trabant (Satellite) ride, and also carried the power sets.
Photograph by Malcolm Slater

LEFT: Michael Pullen obtained this Foden S10 Fleetmaster from Robson's Border Transport, Carlisle, to haul his living wagon and Hot Dog Stall. The tractor was originally an artic finished in the livery of United Glass, Castleford and carried the name Border Pageant.
Since this picture was taken on Newcastle Town Moor, the unit has returned to its original specification of an artic unit to haul a Fun House ride. *Photograph by Malcolm Slater*

RIGHT: When Even Moran purchased a Top Spin ride from a Lincolnshire coast amusement park, he also acquired a Foden 6x4 tractor unit to haul it around fairs both in Yorkshire and other parts of the country. Morans also purchased another six wheeler tractor unit which had previously been used by showman Willie Webb, in order to carry the electric power plant for the ride. *Photograph by Malcolm Slater*

LEFT: W. Nichol's one load Dodgem ride with a Foden Fleetmaster tractor unit in charge. The whole ride has been adapted to be carried on one trailer, although the building up of the ride remains the same. Unlike some one load dodgems which are not so labour intensive, the cars are loaded and unloaded onto the top deck via a tail lift.

Photograph by Malcolm Slater

BELOW: A Foden which has changed beyond all recognition is the one owned by John Simons. The lorry started life with a tipper body and dated S10 cab. When John purchased one of the new generation of fold up, one load Galloper rides he set about converting the Foden to pull the ride. The chassis has been shortened and a more modern S10 cab fitted. The Gallopers travel widely.

Photograph by Malcolm Slater

ABOVE: The Dutch lorry building firm FTF started life like DAF, as trailer builders, and ventured into truck building using parts sourced from other companies. There can be no mistaking this Motor Panels cab as used by Seddon and Foden in Great Britain. Dutch showmen frequently attend the big fairs in Northern Ireland. Pictured here is part of a Dutch Roller Coaster load arriving with an FTF 6x2 up front. *Photograph by Phillip Dunnill*

BELOW: Another FTF with Motor Panels cab and Detroit diesel engine. Again it is operated by a Dutch showman and pictured in Belfast, but this time the load is part of a Giant Wheel ride.
Photograph by Phillip Dunnill

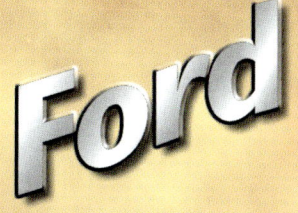

LEFT: Without doubt the oldest working Ford on fairground duties is the Model AA. Built in 1932 it has to be Britain's oldest working commercial. The Ford is in daily use with John Carter's Amusements based in Berkshire. The vehicle is maintained to a high standard and has to undergo an annual MOT test. On moving day the van pulls the organ truck from the set of Gallopers. The side panel opens to reveal a games stall whilst the fair is open. *Photograph by Malcolm Slater*

LEFT: Ford's most successful truck was the D series, and was in production from 1965 to 1981. Many found their way onto the fairground, such as this one operated by A. Gregory. It has been painted and lined out to match the living wagon behind. It is photographed leaving Hampstead Heath in London. *Photograph by Malcolm Slater*

RIGHT: Ford's Transit range of vans are market leaders, popular with parcel delivery companies and public utilities. Many find their way into fairground service. Co Durham based showman Paul Evans operates this ex-Telecom Transit. The original body takes on a whole new look with the added panelling and storage boxes. The brackets on the side of the body carry the legs from the Swing Boat ride. The original petrol engine has been retained.
Photograph by Paul Evan's

Travelling Fair

Ford

BELOW: Largest of the D series was the 28 ton tractor, few of which were used by showmen. Foden and ERF tractors being the preferred units for moving large rides. LAR371V, a Hertfordshire registered tractor, seems quite at home with the Rock o Plane ride in this picture.
Photograph by Richard Laughton

ABOVE: Later D series can be identified by the smaller grill with the small Ford logo in the middle. Stanworth's Fun Fairs did not waste the opportunity of advertising the business and the large body side was ideal for the job. The lorry is pulling a juvenile train ride.
Photograph by Malcolm Slater.

BELOW: Never popular was the Ford K series normal control truck. The cab was built by Pressed Steel Co and early models were badged as Trader. Very few were sold, operators preferring the forward control style of vehicle.
Photograph by Malcolm Slater

RIGHT: Mean machine! Lancashire based showman David Litliernhurnest has the only American Ford CLT-9000. Used to move his show, the aluminium cabbed tractor is finished in black all over with the artist's talent displayed to good effect on the cab side. The tractor was designed to work up to 62.2 tons Gross Vehicle Weight. Its fairground load in Britain is well within the units capabilities. *Photograph by Malcolm Slater.*

ABOVE: Replacement for the D series was the Cargo range. Roger Tuby is one of many showmen who have found the Cargo ideal for moving juvenile rides etc. The one seen here is also fitted with a tail lift and as with all Tuby vehicles the Ford is finished to the highest standard.

Photograph by Malcolm Slater

BELOW: The largest vehicle in Ford's stable was the H-Series Transcontinental, built in the Netherlands. It was built mainly from sourced parts. Towards the end of production the model was built at Foden's plant at Sandbach, Cheshire. Built to operate at the then maximum 44 tons several found their way into fairground service. This one complete with Special Type's General Order plate was used to transport the complete Dodgem load.

Photograph by Malcolm Slater

FWD

RIGHT: The F.W.D. Su-Coe, was used first as an artillery tractor with the British and American armies. Most found favour with British travelling Circuses, Showmen preferred the British A.EC. Matador. Several Su-Coe's did enter fairground service and MPO 749 is one such vehicle and is used by Harris's Amusements. The tractor survives today although it has received a total cab rebuild.
Photograph by Rod Mullard.

LEFT: Photographed on Easter Monday 1970, C. Searle's FWD Su-Coe stands at Wormwood Scrubs, London. As with most Su-Coe's FVB229 carries the lighting sets.
Photograph by Alan Pepper.

RIGHT: The pulling power of the Su-Coe is well represented with this shot of a tractor owned by Rodgers Amusements, Bristol, hauling its load uphill. Rodger's operated several Sue-Coe tractors. The Su-Coe name is short for Short Utility Cab Over Engine.
Photograph by Malcolm Slater.

RIGHT: Traylens Amusements' F.W.D. tractor retained many of its military features including the canvas top. The tractor is fitted with a front mounted crane, which was used in conjunction with the winch rope, to help lift the heavy ride parts.
Photograph by the late A.C. Durrant

LEFT: One of the longest surviving F.W.D.s was the unit of Stanley Thurston. A metal top has replaced the original canvas one and the tractor still has a military look about it.
Photograph by the late A.C. Durrant.

LEFT: Fresh out of military service! This unidentified F.W.D. still has its army number visible on its door. The tractor was photographed at one of the post-war London Fairs in the early 1950s.
Photograph by the late A.C. Durrant.

GUY

RIGHT: West Country showman Tommy Rowlands operated two Guy Invincible tractor units with his Atlanta Dodgem ride. DLU745C seen here, entered fairground service with Whitelegg's Amusements in 1970, before going on to see further fairground service with T. Rowland's. Originally a truck mixer the tractor has been preserved since retirement.
Photograph by Malcolm Slater.

LEFT: Another long surviving Guy, this time an Invincible model, was 431CFJ. Operated in and around the West Country it was still going strong in the 1980s.
Photograph by Malcolm Slater

RIGHT: FM. Gallagher's Guy Invincible eight legger retained its original flat body, for its duties with the Cyclone Twist ride, its owners adding the frame body to it for added carrying capacity. The lorry was operated into the 1980s before being scrapped and replaced by an Atkinson six wheeler.
Photograph by Paul Evens

ABOVE: When Jaguar took over Guy Motors in 1961, the big J Series appeared, the cab produced by Motor Panels. Several Big J 4s survived and entered fairground service. First registered in Eastham London in 1974, this lorry is actually a product of British Leyland who purchased Jaguar in 1968 and continued to produce the Guy J series. *Photograph by Malcolm Slater*

ABOVE: The Dodgem ride of Lancashire showman Glyn de Koning were carried for a short time in the 1980's on this Guy "Big J 8" it is one of the later models featuring the wide grill the lorry was photographed one one of its rare trip's out of its home county over the hill in Yorkshire, with Marshall's fair at Wetherby North Yorkshire. *Photograph by Malcolm Slater*

RIGHT: Another Leyland produced J4. The cab features the later style of large grill. The Luton body has been adapted and cut to suit the chassis, the bottom panel cut to gain access to the fuel tank and small lighting set.

Photograph by Malcolm Slater

LEFT: Arthur Silcock operated this Big J Six in conjunction with his Speedway ride in Lancashire. Photographed in Orford Park in Warrington, the smart box lorry is a long way from its first place of registration with Somerset County Council.

Photograph by Malcolm Slater

Hanomag

RIGHT: A vehicle type rarely seen by British fairground enthusiasts. Dutch showmen are finding their way onto several of our larger fairs and with them come makes of lorry that are strange to our eyes. One such type is the Hanomag-Henschel. Rooper's from Holland have made the occasional trip over to attend fairs and this Hanomag was with the Spider Polyp ride at Bridlington East Yorkshire in the 1980s. It had opened the previous week at the prestigious Hull Fair.
Photograph by Malcolm Slater

BELOW: We return to the giant Hull Fair to see another Hanomag, this time an F66 model. This one came into Britain with a ride operated by Matt Taylor. The Hanomag company was taken over by MAN and Mercedes Benz respectively.
Photograph by Malcolm Slater

Honda

![Honda Acti van with juvenile ride]

Above: At the small end of fairground transport, they do not come much smaller than the humble Honda Acti van. Roger Tuby's Honda body can just accommodate the coin operated juvenile ride. Roger also operated amusement arcades in and around Doncaster, South Yorkshire. The picture was taken at the famous Doncaster St Ledger Race Fair.

Photograph by Malcolm Slater

Land Rover

RIGHT: The four wheel drive Land Rover has found a place with many showmen. Arthur North was quick to put his Land Rover to good use moving the Dodgem paybox from venue to venue. Windows have been fitted to the vehicles sides.
Photograph by Malcolm Slater

LEFT: The name of Corrigan has been synonymous with fairs in Yorkshire for several decades. Several members of the family now operate arcades and amusements on the North Yorkshire coast. Shaun Corrigan has both arcade and seafront parks in Bridlington. This Land Rover was used as a service vehicle for a time in the 1970s. Note the ladder rack that has been fitted for carrying long items of equipment.
Photograph by Malcolm Slater

RIGHT: Bernard Cole & Son operated this short wheelbase Land Rover in the 1980s. Full use has been made of the roof rack, to display the firm's advertising boards.
Photograph by Malcolm Slater

LEFT: Peter Richardson's Range Rover station wagon is an ideal vehicle for moving the juvenile Jet ride. Many showmen have pressed Range Rovers into service to help move small rides and caravans.
Photograph by Malcolm Slater.

Leyland

LEFT: Holland's Leyland Interim Beaver at Nottingham Goose Fair. The lorry was produced immediately after the Second World War. The front cab windows have received a makeover with modern aluminium frames being added.
Photograph by Graham Upchurch

BELOW: The very austere looking Octopus produced in the late 1940s. John Nichols eight legger was used with his Speedway/Waltzer ride until laid up in the 1970s. The lorry is one of the lucky ones and survived long enough to be preserved.
Photograph by Malcolm Slater

LEFT: Walter Jamesons 1940s Beaver. As the model progressed it received wing style trim to the front. Walter's lorry features a room made into the front of the Luton body and greedy boards giving extra loading capacity.
Photograph by Malcolm Slater

Travelling Fair

Leyland

LEFT: As well as building trucks Leyland also had a thriving bus and coach division. Dating from 1936 this Leyland TD4 had been adapted for fairground duties when this photograph was taken. Bus No 134 was one of the famous Burlingham bodied centre entrance buses which are credited with revolutionising the Blackpool bus fleet in the 1930s. Its fairground service was to see it operated in and around North Yorkshire by showman Barry Aisbett.

Photograph by late Robert Mack

RIGHT: Ex WG Alexander & Sons' Leyland bus was converted to a mobile Fish and Chip saloon. As can be seen from the fuel drum and pipe running to the engine fuel pump, the engine was being used in conjunction with a dynamo to provide electricity.

Photograph Glen McBirnie collection.

LEFT: This Leyland Titan Double Decker received a very severe cut down for its working days on the tober. The bus is ex-Southdown UF7185. The straight towing bar fitted to the front could point the way to the bus having engine problems and it could be nearing the end of its working life.

Photograph Glen McBirnie collection

LEFT: The H registration plate on Billy Bedford's Leyland Comet gives no clue to the lorry's true age. Dating from the early 1950s the lorry was part of Leyland's internal fleet and thus unregistered. It was retired towards the end of the 1960s, when it was purchased for fairground service and subsequently registered for the road.
Photograph by Malcolm Slater

LEFT: John Farrar's 1950s Octopus transported part of the Waltzer ride well into the 1980s, before being scrapped. It also pulled the juvenile ride as can be seen in this picture taken in Peel Park, Bradford.
Photograph by Malcolm Slater

LEFT: A Leyland Comet from the late 1950s seen at Newcastle. The cab was of all steel construction and known as the Vista-Vue. It was produced in a joint venture with Albion and Dodge. 5607UP is towing a small juvenile train ride.
Photograph by Malcolm Slater

Leyland

RIGHT: Teesside showman Tommy Leng operated this former removal van. The coach built body fitted to a Super Comet chassis and the lorry's own engine was used to power a generator for the stall lighting. The exhaust was directed through the front bumper and up and away over the fair. The lorry was replaced by a Bedford KM in the early 1980s.
Photograph by Malcolm Slater

BELOW: Possibly the last working L.A.D. cabbed Octopus in Lancashire, Sedgwick's Leyland travelled far and wide and made forays into Yorkshire and Teesside. The vehicle was first registered in Cheshire in 1964.
Photograph by Malcolm Slater

ABOVE: The Leyland Clydesdale was a very popular vehicle with showmen. The Clydesdale was originally a product of Albion trucks, who Leyland purchased in 1951. The cab was a product of the old BMC Company who had also been taken over by Leyland in 1968. The cab was known as the G. This elderly Clydesdale seen at a London fair has suffered some front end damage, presumably sustained when trying to connect the drawbar for shunting the trailer or living wagon. *Photograph by Malcolm Slater*

BELOW: The FG cab was first introduced by BMC in 1959. It survived with Leyland to become the part of the Redline range lasting into the 1980s. This one pictured at Cambridge carries a small Fun House.
Photograph by Malcolm Slater

ABOVE: At the lighter end of Leyland's truck products was the Boxer. It was part of the Redline range and featured the now standard smaller G cab. Jimmy Monte was operating this 1973 model at Newcastle Town Moor Fair in the 1980s.
Photograph by Malcolm Slater

LEFT: Enter the Ergo cab. Introduced in the 1960s the cab was to stay in production with minor style changes into the late 1970s. This 1969 Super Comet thinks it is an Albion, proudly carrying the Albion badge upfront when photographed at Heath Common West Yorkshire.
Photographed by Malcolm Slater

Leyland

ABOVE: This Ergo cabbed Octopus had just entered fairground service when it was photographed on Wanstead Flats, London. The centre mounted crane gives a clue to its previous life as a Brick/Block carrier. The rear mounted tail lift was probably added by the showman to aid the loading of Dodgem/Waltzer cars.
Photograph by Malcolm Slater

BELOW: The Leyland T45 Roadtrain series has found favour with showmen. Yorkshire showman Des Stanley uses this 1985 model with his one load Speedway ride. The ride was purchased from another Yorkshire showman and upon acquisition was adapted to the one load format, the trailer forming part of the ride centre. Des Stanley is well known in and around Yorkshire, for having rebuilt platform rides to one load configuration for several showmen and also for rebuilding Waltzer centre trucks to conform to today's vehicle laws.
Photograph by Malcolm Slater

ABOVE: With a plentiful supply of modern lorries, buses on the fairground are a rare sight. However it is still possible in the 1990s to find one or two still operating with showmen. Hill's Amusements based in Lancashire, use this ex Bolton Corporation Leyland Atlantean as the base for the Museum of Oddities Show. The bus travels far and wide and has been seen in Scotland and down country as far as South Devon.
Photograph by Malcolm Slater.

ABOVE: Heavyweight roadtrain! Joseph Pullen's T45 was new to Warcup Transport in East Yorkshire, and was later sold on to an owner-driver in the Wakefield area before coming onto the fairground. The tractor is hauling a basketball game and small supply trailer.
Photograph by Malcolm Slater

LEFT: Leyland's Marathon range was launched in 1973. It was a heavy weight truck designed for 32 - 44 ton weight range with the cab based on the Ergomatic. The truck was really too large to find any favour with showmen and as a result, finding a Marathon in the entertainment business was a rare sight. The one pictured here was attendant at Hampton Court Easter Fair, London.
Photograph by Malcolm Slater

Living Wagons

BELOW: Many living wagons underwent various changes during their lives. Often, this is more visible inside, where original paintings and ceilings are covered in Formica. This wagon with lantern roof, probably built by Brayshaws of Yeadon near Leeds, was designed to be transported by either road or rail. It has probably been extended at some stage, and has had a side kitchen added. The aluminium exterior possibly covers its original mahogany panels. It has also been mounted on a modern chassis.
Photograph by Malcolm Slater

ABOVE: By the very nature of his business the travelling showman's home has to be mobile. Over the years the living wagon has developed from horse drawn to today's American Hi Line models. This early two room wagon still retains its wooden underworks and front lock, although the original wooden wheels have been replaced by pneumatics.
Photograph by Rod Mullard

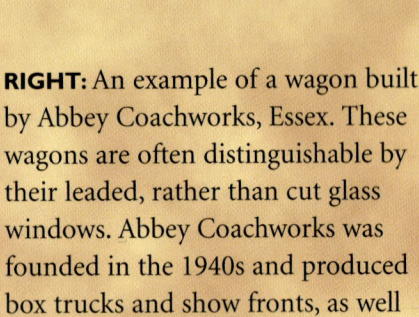

RIGHT: An example of a wagon built by Abbey Coachworks, Essex. These wagons are often distinguishable by their leaded, rather than cut glass windows. Abbey Coachworks was founded in the 1940s and produced box trucks and show fronts, as well as living vans.
Photograph by Malcolm Slater

ABOVE: Another product of Brayshaws of Yeadon, this wagon had been owned by showman Charlie Shaw. However when it was photographed here it had been preserved and was seen at Masham, North Yorkshire where it was used during the filming of a Yorkshire Television drama *"A Day in Summer"* which revolved around the visit to the town Fun Fair.
Photograph by Malcolm Slater

LEFT: A Brayshaw wagon which was well known for many years as the residence of Harry and Priscilla Lee, who travelled the Steam Yachts. It was new in the 1920s to Cilla's family, the Waddingtons, and is still in existence under the ownership of Fred Coupland.
Photograph by Malcolm Slater

LEFT: A wagon in the style of Orton & Spooner was for many years the residence of Harry Holland who travelled a Cake Walk ride. It was photographed at Doncaster, South Yorkshire on the Town Moor Race Course.
Photograph by Malcolm Slater

Living Wagons

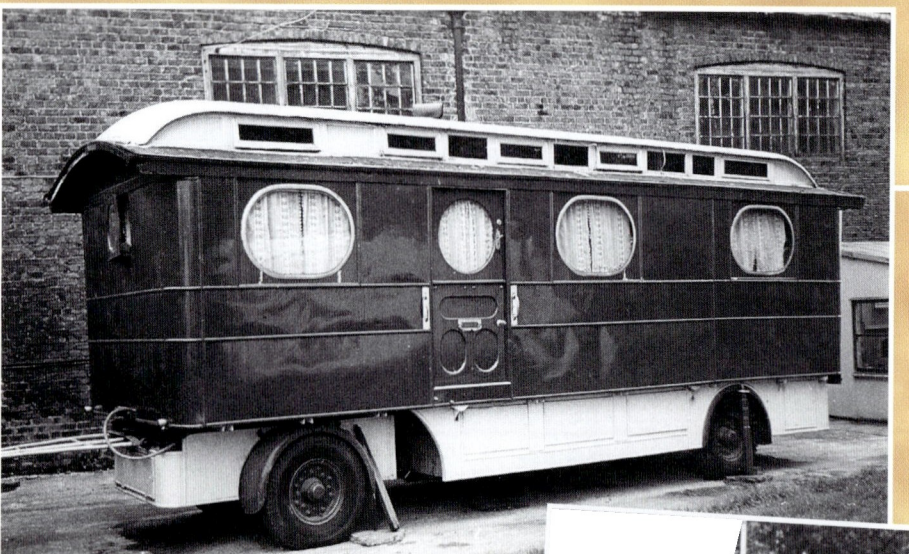

LEFT: Another Brayshaw wagon, this one was once owned by the Tuby family. It was retired to Burton Constable Hall for many years before being acquired by Hull City Museums. It has since been restored but is currently in store.
Photograph by Malcolm Slater

RIGHT: Formerly used by Shipley's Amusements this wagon was spotted in a field near York, where it was being used by a gentleman who was building a new bungalow and living in the wagon until the dwelling was completed. The wagon was later spotted advertised for sale in an estate agents window. It is not known if it was ever sold or was dismantled after the bungalow project was completed.
Photograph by Malcolm Slater

LEFT: An early Pilot wagon now in preservation, built at Oakengates in Shropshire.
Photograph by Malcolm Slater

74

RIGHT: The style of the showman's home has changed again in the 1990s. This American import is fitted with all mod cons including a satellite dish. Time will tell if this type of living van ever becomes as popular with the preservationists as did its predecessors.

Photograph by Rod Mullard

BELOW: In the 1970s and 80s living wagons went through a change. Traditional materials used in construction had given way to lightweight metals. This in turn enabled bigger wagons to be produced, complete with pull out kitchens and living rooms. These new style wagons were also fitted with flush toilets and bathrooms. This one was photographed on Woodhouse Moor in Leeds when owned by showman Colin Shaw.

Photograph by Malcolm Slater

Mack

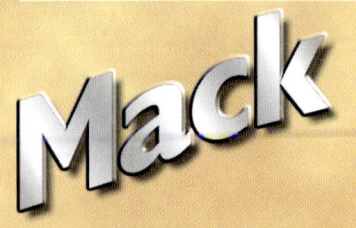

RIGHT: Another ex military show land heavyweight was the American Mack. Most popular was the 6x6 model S. Forrest's LKK101, named The Bat was pictured at Blackheath Fair, London in May 1970.
Photograph by Alan Pepper

BELOW: A World War 2 heavyweight, the Mack was a USA import for the war effort. Many found their way into fairground service in the 1950s. Most were used as haulage tractors and for carrying lighting sets. Bert Holland's vehicle stands on the Forest site at Nottingham. The wooden floor to the right of the vehicle is the floor from Keebbles' Swirl Ride.
Photograph by Stan Savage

ABOVE: Shufflebottom's Amusements operated several Mack vehicles. Mack NM EAJ110 had already been used as a gritter/snowplough before being acquired for fairground service. The tractor still carries the fittings for a plough on the front. Most showmen replaced the original petrol engine for a more economical diesel unit. The American Mack came to England under the lease-lend arrangements made during the Second World War. Production ceased in 1943.
Photograph by Stan Savage

LEFT: Nottingham Goose Fair and a Mack generating tractor stands waiting for the fair to open. The tractor had originally been fitted with a canvas cab. The showman owner has constructed his own hard top using what looks like a car windscreen. Note the very large rear view mirror fitted to the driver's side.
Photograph by Stan Savage

Mercedes Benz

LEFT: The German firm of Mercedes-Benz is one of the world's largest builders of cars, trucks and coaches. They have been selling vehicles in Great Britain since 1928. The LP range of trucks was introduced in 1965 and remained in production until the 1980s. At the smaller end of the "LP" range was the LP809. W. Laytham is seen here pulling onto the sports field at Stokesley, North Yorkshire for the annual street fair.
Photograph by Malcolm Slater.

RIGHT: The Mercedes 2419 model was available as either a tipper or tractive unit until replaced in 1974.
L. Gray operated a smartly turned out 2419. The chassis could possibly have been a truck mixer. Unlike the smaller vehicles in the range which have their wheels set forward of the cab, the 2419 series has the wheels in a more conventional position.
Photograph Malcolm Slater.

LEFT: The LN2 range replaced the LP series of trucks in 1984. Showman James Holmes, who travels the fairs of South Yorkshire, uses this 1986 registered LN. Attractively lettered it is the support vehicle for James's Arcade.
Photograph by Malcolm Slater.

Mercedes Benz

RIGHT: Mercedes New Generation cab was introduced in 1974. The model 1213 11 tonner was a popular vehicle with breweries amongst others, and many have found a second life with fairground operators. This 1213 was seen at Nottingham at the famous Goose Fair.
Photograph by Malcolm Slater

LEFT: As fairground rides get larger, so the equipment needed to operate them becomes more specialised. Over in Ireland William Bird's Amusements operated a Giant Wheel. When the ride was purchased it came complete with its own mobile crane. The Mercedes 2033 6x4 tractor unit hauls the low loader trailer used to move the crane from fair to fair. The tractor unit also double runs, hauling several of the trailers used to transport the wheel.
Photograph by Phillip Dunnill.

RIGHT: Another of William Bird's rides is the self contained fold up Dodgem track. Up front is one of the Birds' fleet of Mercedes, a model 2354 unit. Most of Bird's fleet of vehicles are lettered up as Euro Show fun fairs.
Photograph by Phillip Dunhill.

Scammell

ABOVE: Scammells Military Pioneer model was made in large numbers for use in the Second World War, it was produced in several forms. Silcocks of Warrington had this smart ex recovery Pioneer with their Waltzer ride which can be seen behind the tractor. Also seen behind the tractor to the right of the picture is one of two Albion Caledonian's which Silcock's were using at the time.
Photograph by Graham Upchurch

BELOW: Scammell's Highwayman model was used by showmen all over the country. Elias Harris made the journey to Nottingham for the Goose Fair on a regular basis with his Octopus ride and tractor The tractor and ride were always maintained to a high standard as can be seen in this picture of the Scammell on the Forest ground. The tractor was stored in Harris's yard for many years, and in 1998 Elias's son Anthony started to restore the tractor. Although not finished it was to be one of the star attractions at the 1998 Goose fair pull on. The tractor can now be seen at many of the fairs on the Pat Collin's circuit.
Photograph by Graham Upchurch

BELOW: Another Scammell product produced for the war effort was the Explorer. Many found their way onto the fairground after military service. Such was their staying power that it is still possible in the 1990s to see an Explorer in service with a showman. Harris's have one such vehicle smartly turned out. The tractor can normally be found around Sussex with the Galloper ride. Note how the towing chain has been painted to match the tractor.
Photograph by Les Freathy

Travelling Fair

RIGHT: Victor Sedgewick's Big Wheel travelled far away from its native Lancashire. In the early 1970s it was a regular attender at the large Harrogate August Bank Holiday Fairs. The Scammell Highwayman used to move the loads was new to Shell Mex/BP Ltd. Regrettably it was scrapped before the preservation movement took off.
Photograph by Malcolm Slater

LEFT: Benson's Amusements of Dorking operated a large fleet of Highwaymen well into the 1980s. The fleet was always kept in immaculate condition. Benson's Fun Fair operate in and around London. The fair was arriving at Kennington park when Scammell Thomas V arrived with one of the large living wagons.
Photograph by Malcolm Slater

LEFT: John Wall's Scammell Pride of Hampshire heads along the country roads at North Waltham with two of the firm's Dodgem ride trailers in 1981. The lack of other traffic adds to this animated scene.
Photograph by Peter Hammond

ABOVE: Showmen had few vehicles purpose built to meet their needs. However Scammell did start development of a vehicle suitable for showmen. The final result was eighteen new Showtracs being built between 1945 to 1948. Many of the tractors were supplied with fitted bodywork and Mawdsley dynamo. Several Showtracs have survived into preservation. One though can still be seen at work, doing the job it was designed for. Delivered in 1946 to West Country showmen Anderton & Rowland Gladiator was chassis number 6190. The Showtrac was returned to Scammells in 1949 for overhaul and repaint, before returning to the West Country. It was also exhibited at the Olympia Fair in London.
Photograph by Richard Laughton

BELOW: Some Showtracs still remain with their original fairground owners and one such vehicle is CU4667 chassis number 6111. Named Unique the tractor was supplied in 1946 to Northern Section showman John Powell. Retired around 1962, it reappeared in 1978 for the Newcastle Town Moor Fair sporting a new windscreen, after which it went back into storage. This showtrac is credited with being the only one owned by a northern showman.
Photograph by Paul Evans

LEFT: Scammells set the pace with the introduction of the Routeman 2 featuring a glass fibre cab, and costing around £4,215. Many of the vehicles found favour with petrol and general haulage companies. Tuby's Dodgem track in South Yorkshire used this ex-Shell/BP tanker to transport the tracks principles and cars, the dodgem cars were lifted to the upper floor of the body using a tail lift, the lorry also carried one of the lighting sets.
Photograph by Malcolm Slater

LEFT: Scammell's Handyman range had already had two versions. For the MK3 version the all plastic Italian style cab was used. Many Handyman tractor units found further employment on our fairgrounds both as artics and as generating tractors. Arthur James' Big Wheel is a popular ride travelling around Devon and the West Country. The towing tractor carries two lighting sets side by side. Carrying the name Churchill our picture was taken at Brixham South Devon.
Photograph by Malcolm Slater.

RIGHT: The Crusader 4x2 tractor unit was introduced in 1968 as a 44 tonner designed for heavy haulage work. A smaller 32 ton unit was produced in 1971. The Crusader was never as popular on fairgrounds as most of the other Scammell models. Roland Studts smart tractor was powered by a Rolls Royce 290 unit. Carrying lighting sets the tractor was always smartly turned out.
Photograph by Malcolm Slater

LEFT: John Guest operated two Crusader tractor units, One was used as an articulated unit with the Paratrooper ride. The second vehicle pictured here was used as a towing tractor, hauling the living wagon and Arcade trailer.
Photograph by Malcolm Slater

Scania

BELOW: Scania have been selling vehicles on the British market since the late 1960s.
Yorkshire showman James Southward used this LB111 model and trailer to transport his Twist ride. The ride was later totally rebuilt on its own trailer, and the tractive unit was replaced by a Leyland 4x2 articulated unit. *Photograph by Malcolm Slater*

ABOVE: Dutch showmen often attend the larger fairs in Britain. This Scania 111 left hand drive was photographed at the giant Hull Fair in October.
Photograph by Malcolm Slater.

LEFT: The GPR Range was introduced in 1981 onto the British market, with an all new design of cab. Several have entered fairground service. This attractive 6x4 generating tractor sports chrome wheel trims. The vehicle is a G82M 16.2 ton model and the M Suffix stands for Medium Duty.
Photograph by Malcolm Slater

RIGHT: One of the big boys in Scania's GPR range is the R142H tractive unit fitted with a 14.2 litre engine. This Dutch registered 6x4 artic attended Hull fair with a Top Spin ride. The H suffix stands for Heavy Duty.
Photograph by Malcolm Slater

LEFT: A rare vehicle to British eyes is the Scania 76 Normal Control model. This 4x2 tractor attended the Belfast (Ireland) Christmas Fair. The lorry and load had travelled over from Holland with a Looping Roller Coaster ride. Some of the track parts of the ride can be seen on the trailer.
Photograph by Phillip Dunnill.

RIGHT: The largest vehicle in Scania's British portfolio is the bonneted T range. There is only one model in the range available in Britain which is designated T142E. It is sold as a heavy haulage tractor to work up to 178 tons gross. J.E. Manning and Sons pressed this 6x4 tractor into service. Running on a Q plate the tractor is immaculately turned out. As well as operating rides, Mannings also buy and sell rides and are responsible for importing many thrill rides into the UK.
Photograph by Richard Laughton.

Seddon

LEFT: Seddon Vehicles have been building trucks since the 1930s. Many of Seddon's products have found a second life in fairground service. Seen at Northallerton May Fair in 1974 this four wheel box lorry first registered with Cumberland C.C. was being used to transport a set of joints (Side Stalls).
Photograph by Malcolm Slater.

RIGHT: Yorkshire showman Maurice Waddington travelled this four wheel Seddon box lorry around the Yorkshire fairgrounds. The lorry was on home ground in Yorkshire having been first registered in Hull in the mid 1950s.
Photograph by Malcolm Slater

LEFT: Tuby's Amusements South Yorkshire travelled this Seddon DD8 well into the 1980s. The tractor carried lighting sets and also the Punch Ball coin operated novelty which can be seen standing at the rear of the cab. The lorry was new to the British Sugar Corp as a tanker. It had been laid up with a defective engine, but has since been purchased for preservation and has been restored as a tipper vehicle.
Photograph by Malcolm Slater

Travelling Fair

Seddon

RIGHT: Seddon's first fibreglass cabs were introduced in the early 1960s. Coles Amusements of Southampton had this 1966 Seddon 30/4/6LX in the fleet well into the 1990s. Originally a 30 ton tractor unit, it carried lighting sets, and was kept in immaculate condition as can be seen from this photograph.
Photograph by Malcolm Slater

RIGHT: Crows Amusements based in Northallerton, North Yorkshire commissioned this Seddon artic unit to haul their Meteorite ride. The ride was later to be fitted with a front dolly and the tractor converted to a towing tractor carrying generators. It stayed with Crows well into the 1990s.
Photograph by Malcolm Slater

BELOW: Tommy Peel had this 1968 Seddon in his fleet during the 1970s. The model 13/4 features an all steel cab built by Motor Panels. The 13/4 designation stands for 13 ton, 4 wheeler. The lorry was first registered to Whitby Oliver Removals of York. Seen here at Harrogate Stray Fair the lorry was scrapped in the late 1970s.
Photograph by Malcolm Slater

ABOVE: The fairground in Brixham, South Devon Access is via a steep hill complete with hair pin bend and not at all suited to fairground vehicles and trailers, yet the showmen provide the Regatta Fair every August. This early 1970s registered Seddon tractive unit wends its way up the hill and on to the tober with living wagon in tow.
Photograph by Malcolm Slater

Seddon Atkinson

RIGHT: In 1970 Seddon took over Atkinson trucks but the marriage was only to last four years until the Seddon/Atkinson business was acquired by the American International Harvester Corp. New models were introduced in 1975. The new 200 series featured an all new Motor Panels cab. The 200 series was designed for 14-16 tons making them an ideal chassis for fitting a Fun House body as can be seen on his 1977 model on Wanstead Flats in London.

Photograph by Malcolm Slater.

LEFT: Richard Walton commissioned this 400 series to work with his Waltzer/Speedway ride. Lighting sets were fitted front and rear. Later on the lorry was fitted with a full frame body and lined and lettered out. The 400 series had a choice of engines including Gardner, Rolls Royce and Cummins.

Photograph by Malcolm Slater

RIGHT: Cambridge Mid Summer Fair and C. Gray's Seddon Atkinson arrives with the family home. The 1979 registered 300 series is fitted with the grill from the improved 301 model. Notice also the old Atkinson A badge fitted to the grill. Many drivers favoured the old Atkinson logo for their vehicles. The old A badge was dropped by Seddon Atkinson when the new range of trucks was introduced. This unit is powered by a trusty Gardner 180 unit.

Photograph by Malcolm Slater

LEFT: In the early 1980s Seddon Atkinson launched the 201/301/401 series. The new range shared the basic cab design of the 200/300/400 series vehicles but could be distinguished by the large rectangular grill. It was not long before operators discovered that the new style grill would fit the old cab, in a similar manner to the grills on ERF's A series. Seen with a Twist ride at Cambridge this T reg 300 series sports the new grill, which was introduced some three years after the lorry was first registered.

Photograph by Richard Laughton

Shelvoke

ABOVE: A unique fairground vehicle in the 1990s, this Shelvoke four wheel box lorry OTM891W was put into fairground service by showman James Dean. The lorry was one of a batch of 22 built by Shelvoke of Letchworth to the order of Anglian Water. They all were 4x4 drive and equipped with water tanker bodies. The cabs were a standard Motor Panels product as used by Fodens and others. Anglian Water intended the vehicles to replace Bedford TM's which were no longer available. Jimmy Dean purchased the lorry as a chassis cab, fitting the body and generators himself. The lorry has since been sold on to another Midlands Showman namely Simon Vaugham of Haymills, Birmingham.

Photograph by Malcolm Slater

Thornycroft

ABOVE: Notts and Derby Section showman Charles Holland operated this 1959 Thornycroft Swiftsure well into the 1980s, and it is very possible that it was the last working Thornycroft being used by a showman. The lorry was first registered to the Nottingham firm of Gimson & Slater. It still survives out of use and at the time of writing has been offered for sale for preservation.
Photograph by Malcolm Slater.

Volvo

RIGHT: Volvo trucks have been available in Britain since 1968 and one of the first models was the F86. Built in Sweden and equipped with a Volvo TD70 engine, the lorry was available within the 24 to 32.5 ton range. A Volvo F86 on fairground duties was a rare find as Britain still had a thriving truck building industry. This six wheeler was spotted on the club car park at Hull fair, and was used to transport a Super Bob ride.
Photograph by Malcolm Slater.

LEFT: Steven's Amusements' fleet of vehicles consists of several Volvo units both in rigid and artic styles. This elderly F88 model looking immaculate in its striking red/yellow/green livery was used as a 6x4 generating tractor and was photographed hauling the Waltzer centre and car truck. It was registered in Bedfordshire during the 1973/74 period.
Photograph by Richard Laughton.

LEFT: A Volvo F88 artic of 1976 vintage equipped with a fifth wheel coupling the tractor is hauling a Paratrooper load. The tractor unit has received some customising by its owner, note the air horn, roof rack and chrome wheel discs.
Photograph by Richard Laughton.

RIGHT: Another Volvo from the Steven's fleet, this time Volvo ALC838S. An F12 model 6x4 tractor unit fitted with silent generator across the back of the cab, it is seen with the firms Twist ride. Stevens also manufactured Twist rides such as the one illustrated above, for showmen and theme parks around the world.

Photograph by Richard Laughton.

LEFT: Bob Wilson Amusements are synonymous with fairground entertainment. They are one of the leaders in introducing new rides into this country, travelling far and wide around Britain. For several years they put on a large fair at the Meadowhall shopping complex in Sheffield, South Yorkshire. The cars for the Enterprise ride were carried on this Volvo F7 model. Volvo's F7 was similar to the F6 and was the replacement model for the F86.

Photograph by Malcolm Slater.

ABOVE: Mark Thurston's Break Dance ride has long been popular with the public. More unusual was the Volvo F12 used to transport the ride from fair to fair. The left hand drive tractor unit operated on a Q plate. It was formally operated by a haulier on overseas work and was imported and registered in Britain hence the Q suffix. The ride was later sold on to showman Freddie Stokes without the tractor. Mr Stokes rebuilt the ride floor, which made it possible to carry the paybox on the swan neck. The ride was again sold in 1999 and is now in Australia.

Photograph by Richard Laughton.

ABOVE: A striking Volvo F10 towing tractor unit, operated in Ireland by Barclay's Amusements. Lettered and lined out in full fairground style the lorry carries the name Matchbox which presumably stems from the compact body on the back.

Photograph by Phillip Dunnill.

RIGHT: Another Volvo and the only one to see fairground service on a British fairground. This bonneted artic unit together with Twist ride was photographed at Cambridge where it was a regular visitor at the Mid Summer Fairs in the 1980s.
Photograph by Richard Laughton.

LEFT: The FL10 range was the low cab replacement for the F7. The cab resembles the cab used on Scania's GP range. The FL10 has found great favour with showmen and the model can be seen on most fairgrounds. This 1986 eight wheeler, complete with Fun House load still bears its previous owner's name in the light box above the cab. The front mud flaps added by its showman owner, add an air of distinction to the lorry.
Photograph by Malcolm Slater.

RIGHT: The FH range was introduced by Volvo in 1993 after a large investment programme costing ver £600 million. Keith Emmett & Sons build fairground rides for the world market as well as operating rides in their own right on British fairgrounds. The firm have had this tractor from new. When purchased Emmetts specified that the unit should be finished in a shade of green not normally available on Volvo trucks. The lorry is seen here on home ground at Milton Keynes with the fold up Waltzer ride.
Photograph by Richard Laughton.

LEFT: The normal control N10/N12 range of trucks was aimed at the heavy haulage business. Several have found their way into fairground service, mostly as generating tractors. This N10 six wheel generating tractor was used by Lancashire showman Tony Litliernhurnest with his Tagada Bounce ride well into the late 1990s. The tractor was new to Hargreaves Tankers of Rothwell, Leeds.
Photograph by Malcolm Slater.

Credits

This book has been enhanced by the inclusion of photographs from the collections of the undermentioned whose input has been greatly appreciated.

Bill Brian. Ernest Brown. Phillip Dunnill. Paul Evens. Les Freathy. Peter Hammond. Richard Laughton. Glen McBirnie. Rod Mullard. Alan Pepper. Paul Redfern. Kevin Scrivens. Stephen Smith. Pete Tei. Rod Spooner. Graham Upchurch.

Want to know more?

If you would like to know more about Fairs and the Fairground scene, you can join the undermentioned clubs which cater for the enthusiast and showman alike. Both produce magazines four times a year as well as holding shows and exhibitions.

Membership details can be obtained from:

The Fairground Society
6 Beck Bank
Quadring Fen
Spalding
PE11 4RA

The Fairground Association
29 Mill Street
Belper
Derby
DE5 1DT

If you are researching a fairground subject the National Fairground Archive in Sheffield could possibly help you. Contact:

Dr Vanessa Toulmin. National Fairground Archive. University of Sheffield Western Bank. Sheffield   S10 2TN

The tables are turned!

The author (centre) together with fellow enthusiasts Philip Dunnill (left) and Bob Wilson (right). The picture was taken by showman Tommy Green who decided that it was time that the photographers should be photographed. In the background are Tommy's Flying Coaster and Leyland Octupus lorry.

Pictured at the 1992 Preston Guild fair.

Photograph by Tommy Green